Liminal

21-poems

Andy Havens

BookLeaf Publishing

India | USA | UK

Made with ❤ on the BookLeaf Publishing Platform
www.bookleafpub.in
www.bookleafpub.com

Dedication

For my online friends, who I met between here and there.

Preface

I'm not sure poetry books should have a preface. And if they do, I'm entirely sure they shouldn't address the theme or topic of the book, if there is one. So here's the preface --

Don't linger in doorways for too long.

Acknowledgements

My thanks to the Phoenicians.

1. Bookmark

Simple cardboard
promo item from the shop
where you bought fancy teas.

Orange, too bright, in my view,
wedge-bent
against the shelf above.

I pulled it out. Didn't think,
because it bugged me...
sticking up.

Too late, I realize:

"I could have known
where you'd last touched
these pages."

2. Math

Slow food, fast staff. Our waitress

>   slides like a drift racer
>   juggles six beers
>   makes plates disappear
>   sleight-of-hand with the check

So good she's transparent.
Friendly fun, poised,
perfect timing, so accurate.

Splitting the check, I know you aren't

>   happy. You're mad,
>   mad at work mad at friends,
>   mad at family
>   and shit. All the shit.

I wave you away. Say,

"I'll get the tip."

3. Breakfast

If I time it just right
the bagel pops from the toaster
just after I take my meds
just after I stir my iced coffee
just after I pour my juice
just after I get out the glasses
just after I put in the ice
just after I mix water and cold brew
just after I run the water to get it cold
just after I come down
sore and still tired, on just 5 hours of sleep.

If I time it just right
the bagel pops from the toaster
just after
    I spend 35 years   working in cubes just after
    sixteen years of education just after
  playing in the mud of mom's garden
    with my best friend, digging holes,
    filling them with water, getting
    dirty, making noise
    while mom watches and laughs
I come down
sore and tired, on just 5 hours of sleep

4. Judge

Her dog is so quiet. She
waits like a princess
atop the small hill
at the edge of the park.

She watches the frisbee,
she squints in the sunshine,
but I know she's waiting
just waiting to bark.

A hound will offend or
chihuahua will stray or
dachshund streak by
on tiny, twee paws.

And then: she erupts!
with bright, righteous anger.
She yells, "Hey! You! Moron!
There should be a law..."

5. Nametag

"The map is not the territory... the word is not the thing."
- Alfred Korzybski

- - -

Thirty years ago.

Welcome to the conference.
I'm from Ohio, you're from Texas.
They put our home states on our nametags.
Ice-breaking.

We wait in line for the "full breakfast."
One of us says,
"What makes it full is bacon."
The other of us chuckles.

One of us is named
Aaron or Andy or Alan or Ashton or something.
The other of us is named
Shelly or Sheila or Shelby or Sharon or something.

We both take bacon.

A lifetime later, I do not remember your name
or why I was at that event or even what state it was in
(since the conference did not have a nametag).

But I remember that you were from Texas.
That you chose your bacon very carefully,
like an artist picking colors from a box of expensive
pencils.

6. Paths

Grass worn down to hard, bare dirt.
Twelve janky lines sketched
on the quad.

Another twelve are gray,
paved, neat. They meet
like hired, well-trained guards.

Everyone I ever loved
I men on worn, dirt, random
strands.

7. Dragon

You don't want me
in the kitchen
while you cook.
Even if I stay at the table
well away from the alchemy.
Even if I stay silent
as I read a random book
I found in the basement.
Even if I avoid all eye contact,
sit with my back to you,
put on my headphones,
look out the window,
stare at the birds,
think about baseball.

You don't want me
in the kitchen
while you cook.

And I don't want you
to read my poetry.

8. Dock

Weekly river trip canoeing
with my father and my brother,
Sundays down the Charles River,
out and back from Redwing Bay.

Every week we pass the landmarks:
mossy boulder, giant willow.
Every week we pass the ruins
of a wealthy, failed estate.

Sadly slumped, the hunchback mansion.
Flooded wreck of riches past.
Grassy lawns now choked with rushes
hiding fences' broken teeth.

Sadder still the length of timber
poking out into the flow.
Planks and pillars rotted, weeping
rope and clots of rusted nails.

Modest lumber, small dimensions
only good for pleasure craft.
Rowboat, kayak, dory, skiff,
and canoes for lazy Sundays.

Bones of summer, bones of wealth.
We strap ours to the family van.

9. Summer

Highways at night are prayers.

If they are fast and dry and free of traffic.
If they wind comfortably through the countryside,
caressing rural towns along the way...
If you turn the music off and feel
the hum and chuckle
of the pavement...

then your prayer is prioritized.

We didn't have a destination, that summer.
Just two weeks between end of classes
and start of seasonal employment.

We had $450 between us
and a 1981 Toyota Corolla
and a box of mix tapes
and all the hormones.

We both still smoked that summer,
buying cartons of whatever
state liquor stores sold cheap.
We hung butts out windows,

blew smoke rings,
kissed each other with mouths and lungs
full of bitter, sensual, menthol poison.

The road was our prayer
and the smoke carried it up to the gods
like those swinging, metal bowls
the priests use. Incense
by any other name,
may not provide a rush.
Your mileage may vary.

We knelt on the side of the road,
on the grass or dirt of the breakdown lane.
We knelt to vomit
when we'd had too much to drink
and the light of the daytime trek
was too much.

Driving into the sun is not a prayer.
It is an indulgence.
A contract with some god
much more regular and lawful
than God.

Sometimes sleeping in the car.
Sometimes fucking in cheap motels.

Sometimes finding short-term friends
to share a smoke at roadside picnic tables
or greasy spoons with names like:
"Mom's," or "Twilight Garden," or "The Place."

One week out, in a long, graceful curve mostly north and
west.
One week back, jig-jagging mostly south and east.

No plan. No maps. No itinerary. No journal. No photos.
No meet-ups. No bucket lists. No souvenirs. No t-shirts.
No cell phones. No texting. No group-chats. No internet.
Only

night sky prayers;
day glare nausea.

Two weeks of nothing but two people
two voices
two bodies
two acolytes and

if you held a gun to my head
and asked me,
"What on your resume is a lie?"
What is missing that defines you?
What counts as a terrible omission

on your profile?"

Two weeks. Two voices. Two bodies. Two echoes.

10. Dawn

I resent the new light
this light without choice
that bears down like a threat
like a kid with a sloppy joe
perched on the edge
of a styrofoam plate
coming straight from the parking lot
into the church
from the picnic outside
with the tupperware bins
full of jell-o and beans
and the look on his face
as the sandwich slides off
towards the rug in the narthex
that is the look
it's the look of this sun
staring down on this day
as the mess teeters hotly
before we
must cope
with the mess

11. Courtesy

Why won't you look at children when they play
across the room while we all sit and drink?
The sounds of Lego, puzzles, and a stray
domino or three. Why don't you think

that we can have our wine and fancy cheese
simultaneous to muffled, knee-high din?
So far above them, so displeased
to even let their gnomic laughter in.

Mature? That's not your vibe, I fear.
Just petulant that you have lost those years.

12. Trans

I knew you first as Micha.
Decent student, well behaved.
Introverted, quiet,
several piercings,
green-dyed hair.

You friended me on Facebook,
at the end of the semester.
I was glad, because it's rare
for students to stay in touch.

Twelve years later, you are Emma.
Decent coder, well behaved.
Introverted, quiet,
several piercings,
purple hair.

Same shy and humble smile.
Same green eyes,
same love of puns.

But now you are so different.
Because now
you're in your thirties.

13. Punch

There is no sweat
like middle-school dance sweat.
The gym filled with bodies
but not in our gym clothes.
The court packed with movement
but not from our dodgeballs.
Pheromones thick,
from lust, shyness, and hope...

not thick with the rope-climbing
fear of a fall.

The snack table bent
from decades of service.
The punch bowl a relic
of post world war two.

"Bug juice," we called it.
Cheap, store-brand red sugar,
mixed with a wooden spoon,
served with a cup.

But you let me bring you one.
We drank on the bleachers.

I was James Bond.
And you were Bond, too.

14. Pressure

I am a barometer
made un-cunningly.
A bag of self-cycling liquid
twisted by gravity and weather.
The thing
(that might be me)
living behind my eyes
leans into the storm front,
feels the pulse of our earth
throb and flex outside
the door of the thing
(that might also be me).

15. Midnight

Children fear
the witching hour
because it's fun to
fear a moment that passes
so
quick
ly.

By the time
(time, time, time)
we're old enough to know that
the soul of midnight
shift
s
each night
depend
ing on

|| plans, traffic, partners, chemicals,
wind, tides, location, neon,
vodka, labor, dynamics,
temperature, stress, sugar,
tragedy, socks ||

circumstance,

the witch has
moved in
permanently
and changed the locks.

16. Landmarks

There the crib, now packed away
There the swing, unswung today.
There the schoolyard, empty now.
There the bleachers, draped in snow.
There the back road to the camp.
There the sleeping oil lamp.
There the restaurant for the team.
There the frozen frogging stream.

Here the world that always stays.
Hear the notes that always play.
Here the wish for kinder ways
to pass the years and months and days.

17. Carabiner

I am going to connect two things.
I want you to randomly suggest them.
Can you do that? Truly be random?
Can you suggest two things that aren't

intrinsically connected?

Apple. Stapler.
Communism. Elastic.
Nursery school. X-rays.
Silver polish. Cave paintings.

I don't have to do it.
You, the reader, have already begun.
You want to see the pattern.
Because there's always a pattern.

Because
you
are the shortest distance
between two
[   ]

18. Tempo

the feel of the roll and the road and the rule
of the real, random, reason of recently ruined
by the wail of the whine from the wind and the rain
to be born again, born again, lapsed, born again

for the Nth time it takes to take time with some time
for a moment of limited tension and slide
into ruinous recklessness slippery sand
of the tide of the times of the water, the land

of the random wail roll and the road rule of whine
no more N+1 born again
end
out of
time

19. Larson

LARSON
is carved in deep sans serif
across the face
of the flat, light gray stone.

LARSON
is pleased with its name
on the place
where the dead lay alone.

LARSON
no first name, no dates
is content
to shout as you walk on by.

LARSON
is all we get, waiting
for all of us
under the sod.

20. Petals

In the station of the subway...

An older woman sits reading the paper.
A younger woman scrolls her phone.
The younger woman puts down her phone
and takes a deep, shuddering breath.
The older woman says something.
I imagine she's asking,
"Are you OK?" or "What's wrong, dear?"
But I can't hear
because we're in the station of the subway.

The younger woman waves her hands
drying new tears before they drag race
mascara down her face.

The older woman says something else.
I imagine she's saying,
"It will be OK." Or, "There, there." Or, "Oh, honey."
But I can't hear
because we're in a station of the subway.

The younger woman hangs her head.
The older woman puts a hand on her shoulder.

The younger woman leans a bit closer.

My train arrives.
I leave like a pale ghost
never seen by them, never seen
by the old woman getting out a handkerchief
and the younger woman saying something like,
"Thank you."

21. Intermission

This was a terrible idea.
This is a terrible play.
This is a terrible theater.
The actors are terrible.
I feel like crap.
You are pissing me off.
Let's just go home now.

Or...